The Most Basic Vietnamese

All You Need to Know to Get By

James McGlasson

Copyright © All rights reserved

James McGlasson, 2012

The Most Basic Vietnamese
All You Need to Know to Get By

Acknowledgement
I would like to say a big thank you to Ngọc Ánh Tạ, who patiently checked through this book with me, correcting my mistakes in language and pronunciation, and who helped a great deal.

Aim
This book is meant for those travelling to, moving to or living in Vietnam, and provides all the language you will need to get by while there.

Introduction
Vietnamese is a daunting language to many people, and although it is true that to become truly proficient in the language requires a lot of time and effort, just as with any language, learning enough Basic Vietnamese to get by is extremely easy. Among other features that make Basic Vietnamese easy to learn are the lack of verb conjugation (i.e. the main verb never changes in any tense or for any person), a sentence structure similar to English, and phonetic spellings for words (meaning that once you know how to read each set of letters, you can pronounce everything correctly – unlike people learning English!).

There are far fewer words and rules to learn to get by in Basic Vietnamese compared to European languages too – although the grammar does become a bit more complicated as you learn more advanced Vietnamese, but this book is aiming for the level of exactly what you need to get by – no more, no less.

How to Use this Book

On arrival and for your first couple of days in Vietnam, you will need 'The 10 Most Useful Phrases for a Newcomer'.

Then, with just the language in the rest of the book, you can easily survive in Vietnam for an extended period of time. You can move on in your own order – you may choose to focus on getting the pronunciation basics first, in which case, see the chapters on tones and pronunciation, or you may decide to just dive right in with the basic language chapters and phrases and then get to grips with the tones as you learn more (since using the correct tones is not vital to be understood). Either way will work.

The language is presented in both **English** (in **Bold**) and *Vietnamese* (in *Italics*) with a pronunciation guide [in square brackets].

A Note about Transcribing Pronunciation

I have tried very hard to convey the pronunciation with the simplest and most direct sounding equivalents to the Vietnamese. However, some sounds will not be exact since some sounds exist in Vietnamese but not in English.

In general though, the pronunciation guide is as accurate as it can be, and if anything looks too difficult to read, e.g. [mu'uh'y] – read it anyway! Even though it sounds strange to us, this is because Vietnamese has very different sounds to English. Transcribing this is not easy, and the best way to really learn is just to get practising with locals – in my experience, they are more than happy to help you, and I have had a lot of laughs with Vietnamese people while trying out new sounds with them!

As you spend time speaking the language, and by using the pronunciation and tones guides in the relevant chapters, you will be able to move away from my efforts at transcribing the pronunciation and to read the Vietnamese directly, including the tone and pronunciation markers.

- One sound to note is written as 'kh' in Vietnamese and indicated with a capital [H] in the pronunciation guide. This is pronounced like the '-ch' in the Scottish word 'loch', and **not** like an 'h' or a 'k'.

- Where [ow] is found in the pronunciation guide, the sound is pronounced the same as 'ou' in 'out', and NOT 'oe' as in 'toe'.

- I have also included [?] (question marks) where it seems useful for the pronunciation – this is just as an aid when you start out to show some of the tones which are rising (like in questions in English), but you should get to grips with the actual tonal system if you can – see the section on tones.

- The pronunciation used through the book is North Vietnamese (that used in Hanoi) because it is the standard pronunciation, and pronunciation differs from the South. However, there are a couple of major things you can be aware of if you are travelling or living in South Vietnam (e.g. Saigon):
1. For 'r' at the beginning of words, while the pronunciation guide says [z] for North Vietnam, this is pronounced [r] in South Vietnam.
2. For 'd' and 'gi' at the beginning of words, where the pronunciation guide says [z] for North Vietnam, this is pronounced [y] in South Vietnam.

You will find a guide to **pronunciation** and **tones** towards the back of the book.

Table of Contents

1. The 10 Most Useful Phrases for a Newcomer..................... 5
2. Pronouns... 6
3a. Simple Verbs... 12
3b. Verb Tenses.. 14
4. Some Common Nouns.. 15
5. Adjectives.. 17
6. Other Useful Words & Phrases................................. 18
7. Question Words & How to Use Them........................ 20
8. Numbers & Counting... 22
      General... 22
      Money... 24
      Telling the Time... 26
      1st, 2nd, 3rd etc... 28
9. Situational Vietnamese... 29
      In a Bar or Coffee Shop................................... 29
      In a Taxi... 30
      In a Shop.. 32
      In a Restaurant.. 34
10. Basic Conversation Questions & How to Answer Them...... 37
11. More Useful Vocab.. 43
12. Vietnamese Pronunciation................................... 44
13. Vietnamese Tones.. 48
14. A Summary of What You Will Need....................... 51
15. Also Available... 52
16. Final Note.. 53

1. The 10 Most Useful Phrases for a Newcomer

1. **Hello**
Xin chào   [sin chow]

    (Goodbye
    Tạm biệt   [tam bee'et])

2. **Thank you**
Cảm ơn   [gam uh'n]

    (You're welcome
    Không có gi   [Hom gaw zee]   in North Vietnam
    Không có chi   [Hom gaw jee]   in South Vietnam)

3. **Sorry / Excuse me**
Xin lỗi   [sin loy]

4. **How much (is it)?**
Bao nhiêu?   [bow n'yoh]

5. **I'll take this** (can be used in a shop)
Tôi lấy cái này   [doy luh'y guy nigh]

6. **Go to...** (in a taxi)
Đi...   [dee]
e.g. '*Đi sân bay*' – Go to the airport

7. **Do you speak English?**
Có nói tiếng Anh không? [gaw noy tee'uh'ng ang Hom]

8. **Waiter! Check, please!**
Em ơi! Tính tiền!   [em uh'y, ting ti'uh'n]

9. **I don't understand**
(Tôi) không hiểu   [doy Hom hee'oe]

10. **Where is the toilet?**
Nhà vệ sinh ở đâu?   [n'yah vay sin uh doh]

NB: The 2 words below indicate Male and Female, and are used to identify the men's and women's toilets.

        Men: **Nam**   Women: **Nữ**

2. Pronouns

I/me, you, he/she, we/us, they/them, my/mine, your/yours etc.

Pronouns in Vietnamese are very different to English. They are one of the things that people often find difficult when learning Vietnamese, but they are quite easy once you get the hang of them.

If we learn them in 5 basic stages, they are not hard to get to grips with.

A. The 1st Person (I / me, we / us)
B. You Singular
C. You Plural
D. Third Person (He / him, she / her, they / them)
E. Possessive (My / mine, your / yours, etc)

A. The 1st Person (I / me, we / us)

To start with the most basic, the 1st Person is very easy, we have "I" and "We". There is no change between the subject and object in Vietnamese, so there is only one word for "I" and "me", and also only one word for "we" and "us" (which actually translates as simply 'plural I' or 'plural me').

Tôi   [doy]   **I, me**
Chúng tôi   [choong doy]   **We, us**

Examples:
I am English
Tôi là người Anh   [doy lah ng'uh'y ang]

We are American
Chúng tôi là người Mỹ   [choong doy lah ng'uh'y mi'y?]

B. You Singular

This is the most complicated part of learning Vietnamese pronouns. It can be a little daunting but there are just 8 words to learn, and once you have these down, the rest is easy!

What makes this slightly complex is that the word used for 'you' varies depending on who you are speaking to. The Vietnamese don't really say 'you', but they say e.g. 'older brother', 'auntie' and other such terms of address, depending on age and relationship.

So the words are different for each gender and age group. I will list them here, but as I said, please bear in mind that this is by far the hardest part of learning the pronouns, so it is worth learning these 8 words, and you will find the pronouns easy after that.

Addressing Men

Ông	[aw'm]	This is used to address an older man, of about your grandfather's age.
Bác	[back?]	Means UNCLE / AUNT, and is for both men and women, who are about a generation older than you.
Anh	[ang]	This means OLDER BROTHER, and is for men who are less than a generation older than you.

Addressing Women

Bà	[bah]	To an older woman, of about your grandmother's age.
Bác	[back?]	Means UNCLE / AUNT, and is for both men and women, who are about a generation older than you.
Cô	[gaw]	This means AUNTIE, and is used for women 10-15 years older than you. We also use this to a single woman ("Miss").
Chị	[chee]	This means OLDER SISTER, for women a little older than you.

Both Male and Female

Em	[em]	To a younger male or female. This means YOUNGER BROTHER or SISTER.
Bạn	[bah'n]	This means FRIEND, and can be used for people you see as peers.

Examples:

You are Vietnamese (addressing a younger male or female)
Em là người Việt   [em lah ng'uh'y vi'et]

Do you like eating pho? (addressing a man or woman about a generation older)
Bác thích ăn phở không   [back tick an fuh? Hom]

Here is a rough guide to the age brackets:

Age Group	Male	Female
Grandparents age	*Ông*	*Bà*
1-2 generations older	*Bác*	*Bác*
About 10-15 years older	*Anh*	*Cô*
A little older	*Anh*	*Chị*
About your age	*Bạn*	*Bạn*
Younger than you	*Em*	*Em*
Also, use for single women	-	*Cô*

C. You Plural

This is really easy after learning the above. To make the 'you' forms above plural, the only thing you need to do is to add the word, "*các*" [kak] before each one.

So it is basically the same list as above, but with "*các*" added before each pronoun.

Examples:

Các bác   [kak back?]   **'You'** addressing older men or women

Các cô   [kak gaw]   **'You' addressing women up to a generation older than yourself**

Các em   [kak em]   **'You' addressing younger males or females**

The exception is for old men and women – it is more polite to use "*Các bác*" instead of "*Các ông*" or "*Các bà*".

D. Third Person (He / him, she / her, they / them)

To say 'he / him' and 'she / her' is also simple once you know the pronouns given above.

To change them into the 3rd person, it is another case of adding just one word for the singular (he / she), and 2 for the plural (they / them).

For the **singular** (he / him, she / her), it is just a case of taking the relevant pronoun and adding the word "*ấy*" [uh'y] added after it.

Example:
He wants to go (referring to a slightly older man)
Anh ấy muốn đi   [ang uh'y m'wuh'n dee]

The exception is for old men and women – it is more polite to use "*bác ấy*" instead of "*ông ấy*" or "*bà ấy*".

For the **plural**, there are two possibilities – firstly, there is a word, which just means "they" in general, which is used for mixed groups, and can also save a bit of hassle if you can't remember which specific word to use. This word is: "*họ*" [haw].

The other way, to be specific, is similar to he / she, but it also needs the word "*các*" before the pronoun ("*các + pronoun + ấy*") and is used to specifically indicate if 'they' refers to e.g. older men, or young people or whichever is relevant.

Examples:

They are going (referring to a mixed group, using the general word "*họ*")
Họ đi   [haw dee]

They are coming (referring to more than one man a little older than yourself)
Các anh ấy đến   [kak ang uh'y den]

I saw them (referring to younger men / women)
Tôi thấy các em ấy   [doy tay kak em uh'y]

Again, the exception is for old men and women – it is more polite to use "*Các bác ấy*" instead of "*Các ông ấy*" or "*Các bà ấy*".

Note for 'they / them'
We only need to say e.g. "*Các {bác} ấy*" once. Then, once it is established who we are talking about, and we can just use the general word for 'they / them', "*họ*".

E. Possessive (My / mine, your / yours etc)

Showing possession is also very easy and again, involves the use of just one word, "*của*" [gu'wah] ('belonging to'). This word is added before the relevant pronoun.

Note that this comes after the noun unlike in English – so 'my car' becomes 'the car **belonging to me**'. See the examples below.

Examples:
His book ("the book belonging to him")
Cuốn sách của anh ấy   [g'wuh'n sack gu'wah ang uh'y]

Our fish ("fish belonging to us")
Cá của chúng tôi   [kaah? gu'wah choong doy]

My car ("the car belonging to me")
(Xe) ô tô của tôi   [(seh) oh-toh gu'wah doy]

This is yours ("this is belonging to you")
Đây là của em   [day lah gu'wah em]

SUMMARY:

I / me, we / us: *Tôi, chúng tôi*

You (Singular): *Ông, bác, anh, bà, chi, cô, em, bạn.*

You (Plural): ***các*** + ___

He, she: ___ + ***ấy***

They, them: ***họ*** or ***các*** + ___ + ***ấy***

Possessive: ***của*** + ___

3a. Simple Verbs

Verbs are extremely easy to use as their form never changes. Just add the verb to I/you/we etc. If it is clear who is performing the verb, you can even drop I/you/we etc.

Negatives – to include 'DON'T' as a negative, simply add *'không'* [Hom] before the verb (e.g. *tôi muốn* – I want, *tôi không muốn* – I don't want, *tôi nói* – I speak, *tôi không nói* – I don't speak).
To say 'DON'T' as an order, add *'Đừng'* [duh'ng] before the verb (e.g. *Đừng đi* – Don't go!)

Questions – Add the word *'không'* after the sentence (e.g. *Anh ấy thích Việt Nam* – He likes Vietnam. *Anh ấy thích Việt Nam không?* – Does he like Vietnam?)
To make longer sentences (in Basic Vietnamese), it is usually as easy as translating English word for word – **I don't want to go to the airport** = *Tôi không muốn đi sân bay.* **My friend likes watching football** = *Bạn của tôi thích xem bóng đá.*

Be/am/is/are   *là*   [lah]
e.g. *Tôi là sinh viên* – I am a student

Have/has   *có*   [gaw]
e.g. *Có cơm gà không?* – Do you have chicken and rice? (a common dish)

Go (to)   *đi*   [dee]
e.g. *Đi chợ Bến Thành* – Go to Ben Thanh Market (instructing a taxi)

Come   *lại, đến*   [lie], [den]
e.g. *Lại đây!* – Come here!

Go back, come back   *về*   [veh]
e.g. *Anh ấy về nhà* – He's going back home

Want   *muốn*   [m'wuh'n]
e.g. *Tôi muốn đi* – I want to go

Look, watch, see   *xem*   [sem]
e.g. *Xem này* – Look at (or Watch) this

Give   *đưa*   [du'ah]
e.g. *Đưa nó cho tôi* – Give it to me

Speak   *nói*   [noy]
e.g. *Tôi không nói tiếng việt* – I don't speak Vietnamese

Eat ăn [an]
e.g. *Tôi không ăn thịt lợn* – I don't eat pork

Drink uống [oo'ong]
e.g. *Em (muốn) uống gì?* – What do you want to drink?

Cook nấu [know]
e.g. *Bạn có thể nấu kĩ hơn được không?* – Can you cook this a little longer?

Like thích [tick]
e.g. *Tôi không thích Justin Bieber* – I don't like Justin Bieber

Love yêu [ee'oh]
e.g. *Anh ấy yêu bóng đá* [bong dah] – He loves football

Can / be able to có thể [gaw tay]
e.g. *Em có thể bơi không?* – Can you swim?

Need cần [guh'n]
e.g. *Chúng tôi không cần nó* – We don't need it

Must, have to phải [fie?]
e.g. *Tôi phải đi* – I have to go

Ought to, should nên [nen]
e.g. *Em nên xem nó* – You should watch it

Think nghĩ [ngi'ee]
e.g. *Tôi không nghĩ vậy* – I don't think so

3b. Verb Tenses

The basic verb tenses in Vietnamese are easy to learn and use. Each tense simply involves adding in one word to signify either the past, present or future. Before you learn these tenses though, know that in Vietnamese, it is not as necessary to use them as in English unless you want to really specify the tense. Tenses are especially unnecessary when the time / day etc of the event is known, so for example we could say, "I go to school yesterday" instead of "I went to school yesterday" because the word 'yesterday' has already told us it is in the past. Also, for basic understanding, from my personal experience, I didn't learn any tenses for a long time and I was usually understood from the context.

Simple Present Tense (I go)
This is exactly as we learned earlier – it is just a case of using the main verb form.
For example, as we have seen before, **I go** = *Tôi đi*. **I don't go** = *Tôi không đi*.

Present Continuous Tense (I am going)
Here, we add the word '*đang*' [dang] before the verb, and it changes the meaning to 'am / is / are doing'.
For example, **I am going** = *Tôi đang đi*. **I'm not going** = *Tôi không đang đi* OR *Tôi đang không đi*.

Simple Past Tense (I went)
To indicate the past, we add the word '*đã*' [dah?] before the verb.
For example, **I went** = *Tôi đã đi*. **I didn't go** = *Tôi đã không đi*. (Note the position of '*không*').

Future Tense (I will go)
To indicate the future, the word added before the verb is '*sẽ*' [seh?].
For example, **I will go** = *Tôi sẽ đi*. **I won't go** = *Tôi sẽ không đi*. (Note the position of '*không*').

4. Some Common Nouns

People

Friend	*bạn*	[bah'n]

(My friend = *bạn (của) tôi*)

Boyfriend	*bạn trai*	[bah'n ch'eye]
Girlfriend	*bạn gái*	[bah'n zye]

or:

Partner, b/f, g/f	*người yêu*	[ng'uh'y yee'oh]

(literally: "beloved person")

Husband	*chồng*	[chaw'm]
Wife	*vợ*	[vuh]

Police	*công an*	[com an]
Male Teacher	*thầy giáo*	[tay zow]
Female Teacher	*cô giáo*	[gaw zow]

Places

Home	*nhà*	[n'yah]

(To go home = *về nhà*)

Airport	*sân bay*	[suh'n bye]
City	*thành phố*	[tang faw]
Hotel	*khách sạn*	[Hak san]

(My hotel is in District 1 – *Khách sạn của tôi ở quận 1*)

Restaurant	*quán*	[wah'n]
Park	*công viên*	[com vee'uh'n]
Pharmacy	*hiệu thuốc*	[hee'oh too'oc]
Toilet	*nhà vệ sinh*	[n'yah vay sin]

Shop	*cửa hang*	[gu'ah hang]
– **Go shopping**	*đi mua sắm*	[dee mu'ah sam]

School	*trường*	[chu'ong]
– **Go to school**	*đi học*	[dee how'p]

Transport

Car	*xe ô tô (North VN)*	[seh oh-toh]
or:	*xe hơi (South VN)*	[seh huh'ee]
Motorbike	*xe máy*	[seh my]
Bicycle	*xe đạp*	[seh dah'p]
Bus	*xe buýt*	[seh b'weet]
Train	*tầu hỏa*	[doh h'wah]
Taxi	*xe tắc xi*	[seh taxi]
Motorbike taxi	*xe ôm*	[seh ohm]
Cyclo	*xích lô*	[sik-loe]

(Vietnam's version of a rickshaw)

Bus Stop	*bến xe buýt*	[ben seh b'weet]
Train Station	*(nhà) ga*	[n'yah gaah]

(I'm at Saigon train station – *Tôi ở Ga Saigon*)

5. Adjectives

Contrary to English, Vietnamese adjectives are stated right after the noun they describe (i.e. 'a house big' or 'food delicious' – see the examples below).

Big	*lớn*	[luh'n]
Small	*nhỏ*	[n'yaw]
Good	*tốt*	[tot]
Bad	*xấu / không tốt*	[soh], [Hom tot]
OK	*được*	[du'uh'k]
Beautiful	*đẹp*	[dep]
Delicious	*ngon*	[ng'on]
New	*mới*	[muh'y]

Examples

A big house – *một ngôi nhà lớn*

Delicious food – *món ngon (món **này** ngon* – **this** *food is delicious)*

A new motorbike – *xe máy mới*

A beautiful woman – *cô gái đẹp*

6. Other Useful Words & Phrases

Answering Questions

Yes	*có*	[gaw]
No	*không*	[Hom]
Ok	*được*	[du'uh'k]
Maybe / perhaps	*có thể*	[gaw tay]
I don't know	*(Tôi) không biết*	[doy Hom bee'et]
I don't understand	*(Tôi) không hiểu*	[doy Hom hee'oe]
I understand, I see	*Tôi hiểu*	[doy hee'oe]
Sorry	*xin lỗi*	[sin loy]
No problem	*không sao*	[Hom sow]

Modifying

Too (follows adj.)   *quá*   [wah?]
e.g. too (big) = (*lớn*) *quá*

Very   *rất*   [zuh't]
e.g. very (beautiful) = *rất (đẹp)*

Quite   *khá*   [Haah]
e.g. quite (handsome) = *khá (đẹp trai)*

Distinguishing

here	*ở đây*	[uh day]
there	*ở đó*	[uh daw?]
this	*cái này*	[guy nigh]
that	*cái đó*	[guy daw?]
A lot	*nhiều*	[n'yoh]
A little	*ít*	[it]

Time

Today	*hôm nay*	[hohm nigh]
Tomorrow	*(ngày) mai*	[(ng'eye) my]
Yesterday	*hôm qua / hôm trước*	[hohm wah / hohm chu'uh'k]
This week	*tuần này*	[dw'uh'n nigh]
Next week	*tuần sau / tuần tới*	[dw'uh'n sow / dw'uh'n toy]
Last week	*tuần trước*	[dw'uh'n chu'uh'k]
Now	*bây giờ*	[bay zuh]

Place

(to be) at / in / on   *ở*   [uh?]
*(*Tom is at the hotel – *Tom ở khách sạn)*

7. Question Words & How to Use Them

Although there is some slightly more complicated grammar surrounding the use of question words, in Basic Vietnamese, these are relatively easy to use.

Note that some question words are stated before the rest of the sentence, while others come after it – this is indicated for each question word.

What?	*... (cái) gì?*	[guy zee]
Where is…?	*... ở đâu?*	[uh doh]
Who?	*... ai?*	[eye]
Why?	*Tại sao ...?*	[tie sow]
When?	*Khi nào...*	[Hee now]
How?	*.... như thế nào?*	[n'yugh teh now]

(There are many ways to say 'how'. This is one way).

How much (money)?	*... bao nhiêu (tiền)?*	[bow n'yoh (ti'uh'n)]

Examples

How do you eat this?
Ăn cái này như thế nào　　　　　[an guy nigh n'yugh teh now]

What's this? ("Here is what?")
Đây là cái gì?　　　　　　　　　[day lah guy zee]

How can I get to…? ("I go to (this place) how?")
Tôi đến (chỗ này) như thế nào?　[doy den choh nigh n'yugh teh now]

When will you go?
Khi nào (anh) sẽ đi?　　　　　　[Hee now ang seh dee]
OR:
Anh sẽ đi khi nào?　　　　　　　[ang seh dee Hee now]

What do you do / What are you doing?
(Bạn) làm gì?　　　　　　　　　[bah'n lam zee]

Why don't you like him?
Tại sao (em) không thích anh ấy?　[tie sow em Hom tick ang uh'y]

Where is she going?
Cô ấy đi đâu?　　　　　　　　　[gaw uh'y dee doh]

What do you want?
(Anh) muốn gì?　　　　　　　　[ang m'wuh'n zee]

Who is this? ("Here is who?")
Đây là ai?　　　　　　　　　　[day lah eye]

What do you want to drink?
(Bạn) (muốn) uống gì?　　　　　[bah'n m'wuh'n oo'ong zee]

Where do you want to go?
(Bà) muốn đi đâu?　　　　　　　[bah m'wuh'n dee doh]

Where is (Ben Thanh Market)?
(Chợ Bến Thành) ở đâu?　　　　[chuh ben tang uh doh]

How much is this?
(Cái này) bao nhiêu (tiền)?　　　[(guy nigh) bow n'yoh (ti'uh'n)]

8. Numbers & Counting

General
Numbers in Vietnamese are extremely easy if you memorise the first 10.

(0.	không	[Hom])
1.	một	[mot]
2.	hai	[high]
3.	ba	[bah]
4.	bốn	[b'wuh'n]

(There is a second word for 4 – "*tư*" [tugh], which is used in some instances).

5.	năm	[nam]
6.	sáu	[sow]
7.	bảy	[buh'y]
8.	tám	[tam]
9.	chín	[cheen]
10.	mười	[mu'uh'y]

Above 10, the numbers are simply stated as follows:

12	mười hai	[mu'uh'y high]	**"ten two"**
17	mười bảy	[mu'uh'y buh'y]	**"ten seven"**
20	hai mươi	[high mu'uh'y]	**"two ten"**
23	hai mươi ba	[high mu'uh'y bah]	**"two ten three"**
30	ba mươi	[bah mu'uh'y]	**"three ten"**
78	bảy mươi tám	[buh'y mu'uh'y tam]	**"seven ten eight"**

There are 3 small **exceptions**, which are not that important for Basic Vietnamese, because you will be understood without using them, but for those people who will appreciate knowing these:

A. When the number 5 follows the number 10, e.g. 15, 25, 55 etc), it changes from "*năm*" to "*lăm*", basically because it rolls off the tongue much more easily.

15	*mười lăm*	[mu'uh'y lam]
35	*ba mươi lăm*	[bah mu'uh'y lam]

B. For 1 and 11, the pronunciation of *một* remains the same, but for numbers above that, 21, 31, 41..., 321, 571 etc, it becomes mốt – the change is just tonal, and it changes from the 'low-rising tone' to the 'high rising tone'. This is not that important to be understood in Basic Vietnamese though.

C. For 4 & 14, we use *bốn*, including e.g. 400, 404, 514, 4,000 etc. But for other numbers ending in a four – i.e. 24, 34, 44..., 124, 234 etc, we use *tư* instead for 4. Again, for Basic Vietnamese, this is not important and you will be understood whichever word you use.

Larger Numbers

(One) hundred   (*một) tram*   [(mot) cham]

For numbers in the hundreds, 110-199, 210-299, 310-399 etc, are stated simply as "one hundred 10", "two hundred 45" and so on. This is simple, but just note that for the numbers under ten, i.e. 101-109, 201-209, 301-309 etc, we include another word with hundred (which is '*lẻ*' meaning 'odd'), as you will see in the examples below.

429	*bốn trăm hai mươi chin*	"Four hundred two ten nine"
648	*sáu trăm bốn mươi tám*	"Six hundred four ten eight"
999	*chin trăm chin mươi chin*	"Nine hundred nine ten nine"
103	*một trăm lẻ ba*	"One hundred odd three"
909	*chin trăm lẻ chin*	"Nine hundred odd nine"

(One) thousand   (*một) nghìn*   [(mot) ng'in]

Easy Practice
Work out these numbers in Vietnamese: 150, 725, 932, 605.

Money

This section is included just because the figures when dealing with money can get extremely high. The aim is just for you to gain the confidence to say the larger numbers in Vietnamese, since it is very easy to construct them.

So let's go over the larger numbers again and then move straight onto some examples which will show how to say some of the more complicated ones so that you will be able to then state any amount of money that you might need to.

Hundred	*tram*	[cham]
Thousand	*nghìn*	[ng'in]
Hundred Thousand	*trăm nghìn*	[cham ng'in]
Million	*triệu*	[ch'yoh]
Billion	*tỉ*	[tee?]

5,000 Dong　　　　　*năm nghìn (đồng)*

45,000 Dong　　　　*bốn mươi lăm nghìn (đồng)*
   (note that 5 has become *lăm* after *mươi*)

300,000 Dong　　　　*ba trăm nghìn (đồng)*

2,000,000 Dong　　　*hai triệu (đồng)*

30,000,000 Dong　　*ba mươi triệu (đồng)*

10,450,000 Dong　　*mười triệu bốn trăm năm mươi nghìn (đồng)*

To say an amount of money "per" something (e.g. per day, per kg, per person etc).
This is extremely easy – it is just a case of stating the amount of money, as above, and then saying "1 day", "1 kg", "1 person" and so on...

Examples

500,000 Dong per day　　　*năm trăm nghìn (đồng)* <u>*một ngày*</u>

10,500,000 Dong per person　　*mười triệu năm trăm nghìn (đồng)* <u>*một người*</u>

75,000 Dong per kg　　　*bảy mươi lăm nghìn (đồng)* <u>*một kilôgam*</u>

Useful vocab

per ("one")   *một*   [mot]

minute	*phút*	[foot]
hour	*giờ*	[zuh]
day	*ngày*	[ng'eye]
week	*tuần*	[dw'uh'n]
month	*tháng*	[tang]
year	*năm*	[nam]
person	*người*	[ng'uh'y]
kg	*kilôgam*	[kilo-gam]
metre	*mét*	[met]
km	*kilômet*	[kilo-met]

Telling the time

In English, we can either specify the time of day by using **a.m.** or **p.m.**, or we can say '**in the morning**', '**in the afternoon**' or '**at night**'. Vietnamese has something similar to the latter method but where we have these 3 distinctions, morning, afternoon and night, Vietnamese has 5, meaning they are a bit more specific, but they are not hard to learn. All we have to do is follow the time with the following 5 words. The times are approximate, and it is more about getting a sense of what is meant by each one – you can see this in the list below.

In the morning / before lunch (3-11am)	*sang*	[sang]
Around lunch time (11am-1pm)	*trưa*	[chu'uh]
In the afternoon (1-6pm)	*chiều*	[chee'oe]
In the evening (6-10pm)	*tối*	[toy]
At night (10pm-3am)	*đêm*	[dem]

To actually state the time, this is a little bit simpler than doing the same in English. The format for times in Vietnamese includes "o'clock" '*giờ*' [zuh] no matter what the time is. So let's take it in easy steps.

1. The first thing we need to do is state the hour (the number).
2. Then we add the word '*giờ*' [zuh] or "o'clock".
3. Finally we add the minutes – if it is '**past**', then we just state the number. If it is '**to**', then we say 'minus' ('*kém*') and then the number.
4. If need be, we can then add the time of day, e.g. '**in the morning**'.

And that's it – it is very simple, so let's look at some examples.

1:00   "1 o'clock"
một giờ   [mot zuh]

1:25   "1 'o'clock' 25"
một giờ hai mươi lăm   [mot zuh high mu'uh'y lam]

6:50   "7 'o'clock' minus 10"
bảy giờ kém mười   [buh'y zuh kem mu'uh'y]

4:35   "5 'o'clock' minus 25"
năm giờ kém hai mươi lăm   [nam zuh kem high mu'uh'y lam]

and so on…

If we want to say '**half past**' an hour, we simply say the hour plus '(*giờ*) *rưỡi*' [(zuh) zuh'y].

(*rưỡi* = half, so to say 4:30, we really say "4 (o'clock) half")

4:30   "4 o'clock half"
bốn (giờ) rưỡi   [b'wuh'n (zuh) zuh'y]

We can drop the 'o'clock' for short:
bốn rưỡi   (**"4 half"**)

Asking:
What time is it?   *Bây giờ là mấy giờ?*   [bay zuh lah muh'y zuh]
Or: *Mấy giờ rồi?*   [may zuh zoy]

Easy Practice
Work out these times as above:
6:30 a.m., 9:45 p.m., 3:10 p.m.

1st, 2nd, 3rd etc.

For ordinal numbers, all you need is to precede the number with the word *"thứ"* [tugh].

3 exceptions are:
- **1st**, which has its own word not using the number 1.
- **2nd**, which has 2 options.
- And then anything **ending in a 4** – see below.

1st	*thứ nhất*	[tugh n'yuh't]
2nd	*thứ hai*	(or: *thứ nhì* [tugh high / n'yee])
3rd	*thứ ba*	[tugh bah]
4th	*thứ tư*	**not** *thứ bốn*
5th	*thứ năm*	
10th	*thứ mười*	
11th	*thứ mười một*	
12th	*thứ mười hai*	
25th	*thứ hai mươi lăm*	

For 4th, as you will see above, we say '*thứ tư*'. This is just the case for 4th, and anything higher, i.e. 14th, 24th etc, we use *thứ ___ bốn*, just as you would normally expect.

Example
At the 2nd intersection, turn right.
Ở ngã tư thứ hai, rẽ phải   [uh ng'ah dugh tugh high, zeh'eh fie?]

9. Situational Vietnamese

In a Bar or Coffee Shop

Ordering

I want / Give me (no.) bottles of (beer)
Cho tôi (no.) chai (bia)   [chaw doy… ch'eye…]

I want / Give me (no.) glasses of (white wine)
Cho tôi (no.) ly (rượu trắng)   [chaw doy… lee…]

Bring (no.)…
Mang cho tôi (no.) ly (vodka)   [mang chaw doy… lee…]

Numbers
1. *một* [mot], **2.** *hai* [high], **3.** *ba* [bah], **4.** *bốn* [b'wuh'n], **5.** *năm* [nam], **6.** *sáu* [sow], **7.** *bảy* [buh'y], **8.** *tám* [tam], **9.** *chín* [cheen], **10.** *mười* [mu'uh'y]

Drinks

Alcoholic:		
Beer	*bia*	[bee'uh]
White wine	*rượu vang trắng*	[zee'oh vang chang]
Red wine	*rượu vang đỏ*	[zee'oh vang daw]
Rice wine	*rượu gạo*	[zee'oh gow]
Non-alcoholic:		
Mineral water	*nước (khoáng)*	[nu'uh'k (Hwang)]
Coke	*coca*	[koh-kaah]
Orange juice	*nước cam*	[nu'uh'k cah'm]
Lemon juice	*nước chanh*	[nu'uh'k chang]
Lemon soda	*soda chanh*	[so-dah chang]
Hot Drinks:		
Coffee	*cà phê*	[kaah-feh]
Black coffee	*cà phê đen (nóng)*	[kaah-feh den (naw'm)]
Iced black coffee	*(cà phê) đen đá*	[(kaah-feh) den daah]
Hot white coffee	*cà phê sữa nóng*	[kaah-feh su'ah naw'm]
Iced white coffee	*cà phê sữa đá*	[kaah-feh su'ah daah]
Tea	*trà*	[chaah]
Iced tea	*trà đá*	[chaah daah]
I (don't) want ice	*Tôi (không) uống đá*	[doy Hom oo'ong daah]

In a Taxi

Go (to)...   *đi (tới)...*   [dee (toy)]
(*tới* can normally be dropped when using names / proper nouns – e.g. *đi Hanoi*).

In the North
Turn right   *rẽ phải*   [zeh'eh fie]
Turn left   *rẽ trái*   [zeh'eh ch'eye]

(In the South
Turn right   *quẹo phải*   [whale fie]
Turn left   *quẹo trái*   [whale ch'eye])

Go straight   *đi thẳng*   [dee tang]
Stop   *dừng lại*   [zoong lie]

Here   *ở đây*   [uh day]
There   *ở đó*   [uh daw?]
Then   *rồi*   [zoh'y]

Turn around
or **Do a u-turn**   *quay lại*   [way lie]

(At the) intersection / crossroads
     (ở) ngã tư   [(uh) ng'ah tugh]
Turn right at this intersection – *Rẽ phải ở ngã tư này*
At the intersection of... – *ở ngã tư* + 2 street names

Up ahead   *đằng trước*   [dang chu'uh'k]
     (Followed by... "Turn right / left")

Go faster   *đi nhanh hơn đi*   [dee n'yan huh'n dee]
Slow down   *đi chậm thôi*   [dee chuh'm toy]

Asking for Directions:
Where is (Ben Thanh Market)?
(Chợ Bến Thành) ở đâu?   [chuh ben tang uh doh]

How do I get to Ben Thanh Market
Làm sao để đi tới Chợ Bến Thành?   [lam sow day dee toy chuh ben tang]

Example of a Simple Journey:

Hello. Go to Ben Thanh Market. *Xin chào. Đi Chợ Bến Thành.*

Turn left on Le Loi. *Rẽ trái ở Lê Lợi.*

Turn right at this intersection. *Rẽ phải ở ngã tư này.*

…then turn left. *… rồi rẽ trái.*

Ok stop here. Thank you. *Ok. Dừng lại đây. Cảm ơn.*

In a Shop

Price & Bargaining

How much (money)?	*Bao nhiêu (tiền)?*	[bow n'yoh (ti'uh'n)]
100,000 Dong	*Một trăm nghìn (Đồng)*	[mot cham ng'in (daw'm)]
It's too expensive	*đắt quá*	[dat wah]
How about a discount?	*Có bớt không?*	[gaw bot? Hom]

How about (50,000)?
(Năm mươi nghìn) được không?   [(nam mu'uh'y ng'in) du'uh'k Hom]

Asking for Different Sizes & Colours

Do you have bigger?
Có sai lớn hơn không?   [gaw sigh luh'n huh'n Hom]

Do you have smaller?
Có sai nhỏ hơn không?   [gaw sigh n'yaw huh'n Hom]

Do you have another colour?
Có màu nào nữa không?   [gaw moh now nu'uh Hom]

Making Your Purchase

I'll take this	*Tôi lấy cái này*	[doy luh'y guy nigh]
I don't want that	*Tôi không lấy cái đó*	[doy Hom luh'y guy daw?]
Give me the receipt	*Cho tôi biên lai*	[chaw doy bee'uh'n lie]

Money

The Vietnamese currency is called the Dong, and comes in high denominations. To give you some idea, at the time of writing, the exchange rate is roughly 20,000 Dong to 1 US Dollar. While the rate will vary a bit, we can see that things will be priced in thousands, hundreds of thousands and millions of Dong (1 million Dong is equivalent at the moment to about US$ 50).

So while you will find a section on numbers later in the book, it might be useful to include the words here for "hundred", "thousand", "hundred thousand" and "million". There will be more examples in the numbers section of the book.

Also, you normally don't need to include the word "Dong" when stating how much because it is understood.

Hundred	*tram*	[cham]
Thousand	*nghìn*	[ng'in]
Hundred Thousand	*trăm nghìn*	[cham ng'in]
Million	*triệu*	[ch'yoh]

For example,		
1 million Dong	*Một triệu (đồng)*	[mot ch'yoh (daw'm)]
500,000 Dong	*năm trăm nghìn (đồng)*	[nam cham ng'in (daw'm)]

In a Restaurant

Getting a Table
People	*người*	[ng'uh'y]
(How many people?	*Đi bao nhiêu người?*	[dee bow n'yoh ng'uh'y])
(3 / 4 people	*Ba / bốn người*	[bah / b'wuh'n ng'uh'y])

Food
Beef	*thịt bò*	[tit baw]
Chicken	*gà*	[gaah]
Lamb	*thịt cừu*	[tit kew]
Pork	*thịt lợn*	[tit luh'n]
Fish	*cá*	[kaah?]
Vegetables	*rau*	[zow]
Salad	*sa lát*	[sah lat]
Fruit	*trái cây*	[ch'eye guh'y]
(I don't eat…	*Tôi không ăn…*	[doy Hom an…])
(I'm a vegetarian	*Tôi ăn chay*	[doy an ch'eye])
Rice	*cơm*	[kuh'm]
Soup	*súp*	[soop]

Ordering
I want / Give me {1 / 2 / 3…}	*Cho tôi {một / hai / ba…}*
Bring {1 / 2 / 3…}	*Mang cho tôi {một / hai / ba…}*

Bowl	*bát*	[bat]
Plate	*đĩa*	[dee'uh]
Glass	*ly*	[lee]
(this is the normal glass is for rice wine, water, juice etc)		
Glass (esp. for beer)	*cốc (…bia)*	[cop bee'uh]
Bottle	*chai*	[ch'eye]
Can	*lon*	[lon]

Useful Language

Waiter! *Em ơi!* [em uh'y]
(or if they are older than you – *Chị (f) / Anh (m) ơi*)

Check / Bill *tính tiền* [ting ti'uh'n]
(i.e. to request the check / bill: *"Em ơi! Tính tiền!"*)

Knife and fork *dao và đĩa* [zow vah di'ah]
(Do you have a knife and fork? – *Có dao và đĩa không?*)

Spicy *cay* [kye]
(Is this one spicy? – *Cái này có cay không?*)
(I can't eat spicy food – *Tôi không ăn cay*)

Menu *thực đơn* [tuh'k duh'n]
(Do you have an English menu? – *Có thực đơn tiếng Anh không?*)

Example of a simple visit:

"Hello, how many people?" *"Xin chào. Đi bao nhiêu người?"*

4 people. *Bốn người*
...

Waiter! *Em ơi!*

We want 1 chicken with rice, 2 beef phos and one bun bo Hue. *Cho tôi một cơm gà, hai phở bò và một bún bò Huế.*

Bring 4 bowls of rice. *Mang cho tôi bốn bát cơm*

We'd like 4 glasses of beer. *Cho tôi 4 cốc bia.*

Do you have a knife and fork? *Có dao và đĩa không?*

Thank you. *Cảm ơn.*
...

Waiter! Check, please! *Em ơi! Tính tiền!*

Thank you. *Cảm ơn.*

Some Vietnamese Dishes

Pho   *Phở*   [fuh?]
  (rice noodle soup)

Grilled pork with noodles   *Bún chả*   [boo'n chah]
Beef noodle soup from Hue   *Bún bò Huế*   [boo'n baw hway]
Crab noodle soup   *Bún riêu*   [boo'n zi'oh]

Spring rolls (Northern-style)   *Nem*   [nem]
Spring rolls (Southern-style)   *Chả giò*   [chah zaw / yaw]

Bread / sandwich   *Bánh mì*   [bang mee]

Mashed dried shrimps on rice pancake (Central Vietnam)
                                    Bánh bèo   [bang bay'aw]

Vietnamese pancake   *Bánh xèo*   [bang say'aw]
  (crepe filled with shrimp, beansprouts and more)

Shrimp on prawn crackers   *Bánh khọt*   [bang Hot]

Dried rice noodle   *Gỏi cuốn*   [goi kw'uh'n]
  (used for rolling / wrapping)

Rice   *Cơm*   [kuh'm]
Fried rice   *Cơm chiên*   [kuh'm chee'en]
Broken rice (In South Vietnam)   *Cơm tấm*   [kuh'm tuh'm]
Sticky rice (from food stalls)   *Xôi*   [soy]

Vietnamese dessert   *Chè*   [cheh]
  (there are many kinds of *chè*)

10. Basic Conversation Questions and How to Answer Them

It is pretty easy to get by in basic conversation in Vietnamese if you know some basic questions and how to answer them. You will naturally pick up more once you start speaking.

Note that I have chosen (for no specific reason but for the sake of ease) to use the word '*anh*' for 'you' in all of these questions, but this should be amended depending on who you are speaking to.

1. **Where are you from?**   *{Anh} quê ở đâu?*

2. **What's your name?**   *{Anh} tên gì?*

3. **How old are you?**   *{Anh} bao nhiêu tuổi?*

4. **What do you do?**   *{Anh} làm (nghề) gì?*

5. **Where do you live?**   *{Anh} (sống) ở đâu?*

6. **Do you have a wife and kids?**   *{Anh} đã có vợ con chưa?*

7. **Do you like… (Vietnam)?**   *{Anh} có thích (Việt Nam) không?*

8. **How are you?**   *{Anh} khoẻ không?*

1. Where are you from? *{Anh} quê ở đâu?*   [ang way uh doh]
Or: *Quê anh ở đâu?*   [way ang uh doh]

The simple formula to say where you are from is as follows:

I	am	person	(country)
Tôi	*là*	*người*	(…)
[doy]	lah	ng'uh'y	…]

e.g. **I am an English person**   *Tôi là người Anh.*
  You are Vietnamese, aren't you?   *Anh là người Việt phải không?*

A short list of countries alongside the word to indicate the person from each country (If your country is not on here, ask someone when you are there, e.g. at your hotel, how to say it). Many countries are spoken and written the same as they are in English.

Vietnam	*Việt Nam*	[vi'et nahm]
A Vietnamese person	*người Việt (Nam)*	
England	*Anh*	[ang]
An English person	*người Anh*	
USA	*Mỹ*	[mi'y?]
An American	*người Mỹ*	
Canada	*Ca-na-da*	[kah-nah-dah]
A Canadian	*người Ca-na-da*	
Australia	*Úc*	[ook]
An Australian	*người Úc*	
Ireland	*Ai-len*	[eye len]
An Irish person	*người Ai-len*	
Germany	*Đức*	[dook]
A German	*người Đức*	
France	*Pháp*	[fah'p]
A French person	*người Pháp*	
Italy	*Ý*	[i'y?]
An Italian	*người Ý*	

Spain	*Tây Ban Nha*	[tuh'y ban n'yah]
A Spaniard	*người Tây Ban Nha*	
Russia	*Nga*	[ng'ah]
A Russian	*người Nga*	
Japan	*Nhật (Bản)*	[n'yuh't (bah'n)]
A Japanese person	*người Nhật (Bản)*	
China	*Trung Quốc*	[choong wok]
A Chinese person	*người Trung Quốc*	

To state which city you are from, you can say:
Tôi từ ("I'm from") *Hà Nội* (or even *Anh* – England etc).

Or you might hear Vietnamese people saying this:
Quê tôi ở… (e.g. *Viêm Xá*). ("My hometown is…")
This is only used referring to places in the countryside.

Do you speak … (language)? *Anh có nói (tiếng …) không?*

English	*tiếng Anh*	[ti'uh'ng ang]
Vietnamese	*tiếng Việt*	[ti'uh'ng vi'et]
French	*tiếng Pháp*	[ti'uh'ng fah'p]
German	*tiếng Đức*	[ti'uh'ng dook]
Italian	*tiếng Ý*	[ti'uh'ng i'y?]
Spanish	*tiếng Tây Ban Nha*	[ti'uh'ng tuh'y ban n'yah]
Russian	*tiếng Nga*	[ti'uh'ng ng'ah]
Japanese	*tiếng Nhật*	[ti'uh'ng n'yuh't]
Chinese	*tiếng Trung Quốc*	[ti'uh'ng choong wok]

I speak (a little) {Vietamese}
Tôi biết nói (một chút ít) {tiếng Việt}   [doy bee'et noy mot choot it…]

I'm learning {Vietnamese}
Tôi đang học {tiếng Việt}   [doy dang how'p ti'uh'ng vi'et]

No, I can't speak {Vietnamese}
Không, tôi không biết nói {tiếng Việt}   [Hom. doy Hom bee'et noy…]

2. What's your name?   {Anh} tên (là) gì?   [ang teh'n (lah) zee]

My name's Peter
(this is quite flexible, so there are a few possible ways of saying this)

	Tôi tên Peter	[doy teh'n...]
	Tôi tên là Peter	[doy teh'n lah...]
	Tên tôi là Peter	[teh'n doy lah...]
	Tôi là Peter	[doy lah...]

What about you?   Còn (anh)?   [gon ang]

3. How old are you?   {Anh} bao nhiêu tuổi?   [ang bow n'yoh tu'oy]

I am (21)   Tôi (hai mươi mốt) tuổi   [doy (high mu'uh'y mot) tu'oy]

What about you?   Còn {anh}?   [gon ang]

4. What do you do?   {Anh} làm (nghề) gì?   [ang lam (ngeh) zee]

This is where you will have to look up your own occupation – Go online to "vdict.com" and just type it in!

I am (a teacher)   Tôi là thầy giáo (male)   [doy lah tay zow]
Or: Tôi là cô giáo (female)   [doy lah gaw zow]
Or even: Tôi là giáo viên (m/f)   [doy lah zow vi'uh'n]

I am (a student)   Tôi là sinh viên   [doy lah sin vi'uh'n]

5. Where do you live?   {Anh} (sống) ở đâu?   [ang (song) uh doh]

I live in Saigon   Tôi (sống) ở Sài Gòn   [doy (song) uh Saigon]

I live in America   Tôi (sống) ở Mỹ   [doy (song) uh mi'y?]

6. Do you have a wife and kids?
{Anh} đã có vợ con chưa?   [ang dah? gaw vuh gon chu'uh]
  (to a man – can be impolite to ask a woman questions on these topics)

Are you married?
{Anh} đã lập gia đình chưa?   [ang dah? luh'p zah ding chu'uh]
  (also better to a man than a woman)

Note that while the above questions can be taken as impolite by some people, you are likely to be asked them yourself, so be prepared!

I'm single	*Tôi độc than*	[doy doc tuh'n]
I'm married	*Tôi đã có gia đình*	[doy dah? gaw zah ding]
This is my wife	*Đây là vợ tôi*	[day lah vuh doy]
This is my husband	*Đây là chồng tôi*	[day lah chaw'm doy]
I have a boyfriend	*Tôi có bạn trai*	[doy gaw bah'n ch'eye]
I have a girlfriend	*Tôi có bạn gái*	[doy gaw bah'n guy]
I have a b/f, g/f	*Tôi có người yêu*	[doy gaw ng'uh'y yee'oh]
i.e. 'someone I love'		

....

Do you have children?	*{Anh} có con chưa?*	[ang gaw con chu'uh]
I have 2 children	*Tôi có hai con*	[doy gaw high con]
1 son and 1 daughter	*Một (con) trai và một (con) gái*	[mot (con) ch'eye vah mot (con) guy]
I don't have children	*Tôi chưa có con*	[doy chu'uh gaw con]

(Note that '*chưa*' is used instead of '*không*' for the negative here because, in this instance, '*không*' makes it sound like you also don't plan to have children).

7. Do you like… (Vietnam)?
{Anh} có thích (Việt Nam) không?   [ang gaw tick (vi'et nahm) Hom]

Yes, I do   *Có*   [gaw]

No, I don't   *Không*   [Hom]

I love (Vietnam)   *Tôi yêu (Việt Nam)*   [doy yee'oh…]

I like Vietnamese food   *Tôi thích đồ ăn Việt Nam*   [doy tick doh an vi'et nahm]

I don't like (the traffic in Vietnam)
Tôi không thích (giao thông ở Việt Nam)   [doy Hom tick zow tong uh vi'et nahm]

8. How are you?   *{Anh} khoẻ không?*   [ang H'weh Hom]

I am fine, thanks.   *Khoẻ, cám ơn.*   [H'weh. Gam uh'n]

And you?   *Còn {anh}?*   [gon ang]

11. More Useful Vocab

Short Words, Conjunctions etc
And	*và*	[vah]
But	*(bởi) vì*	[(buh'y) vee]
So	*vậy*	[vuh'y]
Or	*hay (là)*	[high (lah)]
If	*nếu*	[nay'oh]
For	*vì*	[vee]
Any	*nào*	[now]

('any' comes after the noun in Vietnamese)

Time Phrases
Always	*luôn luôn*	[lu'on lu'on]
Usually	*thường*	[tu'uh'ng]
Sometimes	*đôi khi*	[doy Hee]
Rarely	*ít khi*	[it Hee]
Never	*không bao giờ*	[Hom bow zuh]
Ever	*bao giờ*	[bow zuh]
Forever	*mãi mãi*	[mah'y mah'y]

Weather
Sunny	*nắng*	[nang]
Hot	*nóng*	[naw'm]
Cold	*lạnh*	[lah'ng]
Raining	*mưa*	[mu'uh]
Cloudy / overcast	*nhiều mây*	[n'yoh muh'y]
Windy	*gió*	[zaw]

12. Vietnamese Pronunciation

(Also look up these two web pages, which have lots of clickable sound files, demonstrating Vietnamese pronunciation: http://www.lovingpho.com/pho-opinion-editorial/pronunciation-vietnamese-words-phrases/
and
http://www.lovingpho.com/pho-pronunciation-menu-ordering/pronunciation-pho-vietnamese-words-phrases-part-2/)

Note that it is not amazingly easy to transcribe Vietnamese pronunciation, partly because some sounds exist in Vietnamese but not in English, and also because the pronunciation varies between the regions. It is a good idea to pay attention to how the locals around you pronounce the words and sounds, and this will give you the best idea of how to pronounce them yourself – of course, the best way to do this is simply by practising with locals.

Pronunciation in Vietnamese can also seem a little complicated for an English speaker, for the following reasons:

Tones
Vietnamese is a tonal language and has 5 tones, with different tones changing the meaning of words.

Pronunciation Markers / Accents
Vietnamese has a few different marks which are placed above letters and change the pronunciation. This makes written Vietnamese appear very complex but, in fact, they are very ordered and there are not that many to learn.

Pronunciation of Letters & Letter Groups
It can be a bit tricky when you begin to speak Vietnamese, because some letters and groups of letters are pronounced differently to English. For example, "-ng" is often pronounced as "-m" while "tr-" is pronounced similar to "ch-". But you will quickly realise where this happens, with just a little experience of speaking, and then it is the same every time.

Although the pronunciation guide below gives the general rules, Wikipedia has an excellent table, which gives the exceptions to the rules (e.g. –ng becomes –ngm after 'u', 'ô', or '–ch' is pronounced as '–t' in Saigon after 'e', 'i', 'y'. This is something you will pick up over time while speaking Vietnamese, but look up the address below if this interests you:
http://en.wikipedia.org/wiki/Wikipedia:IPA_for_Vietnamese

The Vietnamese Alphabet

Vowels

a	'a' in 'father'
ă	'a' in apple
â	'uh' as in the exclamation 'uh'
e	'e' in 'bed'
ê	'eh'
i	'ee' in 'meet' ('i' and 'y' are pronounced the same)
y	'ee' in 'meet' ('i' and 'y' are pronounced the same)
o	'aw' in 'raw'
ô	'o' in 'oh'
ơ	The exclamation 'uhh' or like 'ur' in 'turn' but without pronouncing the 'r'
u	'oo' in 'food', 'oo' in 'book' or 'u' in 'put'
ư	I found this by far the most difficult sound to pronounce – for me, it is similar to a disgusted 'ugh', but it will be useful for you to listen to it yourself and try to repeat it. Look up this address online and you will find a good audio sample of the sound: http://www.forvo.com/word/%C6%B0/.

Consonants

b	'b' in 'book'
p	This is like 'p' in English, but without actually expelling air (it sounds between a 'b' and 'p' to us)
c	This is like 'c / k' in English, but without expelling air (it sounds between a 'k' and 'g' to us)
k	This is like 'c / k' in English, but without expelling air (it sounds between a 'k' and 'g' to us)
ch	Similar to 'ch' in English, but like 'c', 'k', 'p', we do not expel air (it sounds between 'ch' and 'j')

đ	'd' in English – Note, 'd' with a line through it says 'd', 'd' without a line is as below (easy to confuse!)
d	'z' in 'zoo' in North Vietnam, 'y' in 'yes' in the South (Note, **not** as 'd')
gi	'z' in 'zoo' in North Vietnam, 'y' in 'yes' in the South
g	'g' in 'good'
gh	'g' in 'good'
h	'h' in 'hat'
kh	This is like the 'ch' in the Scottish word 'loch' (I have indicated this throughout the pronunciation in the book with a **capital H**.
l	'l' in 'lemon'
m	'm' in 'me'
n	'n' in 'now'
-ng	At the end of a word, this is actually pronounced as an 'm' when it comes after *'u' or 'ô'*, (Note, **not** as 'ng') e.g. *Thang* – pronounced [tang]. *Không* – pronounced more like [Hom]
ng-	At the beginning of a word, this says, 'ng' as in 'sing'
ngh	'ng' in 'sing', just like 'ng-'
nh	'ny' sound in 'onion' or 'canyon'
ph	'f' in 'fancy' or 'ph' in 'elephant'
q	'w' in 'way' (Note, **not** as a 'q')
r	'z' in 'zoo' in North Vietnam, 'r' in 'rice' in South Vietnam
s	's' in 'soon'

t	't' without expelling air, similar to 'c', 'k', 'p' (it sounds between 't' and 'd' to us)
th	't' in 'take'
tr	'ch' in 'chat' (Note, **not** normally as 'tr')
v	'v' in 'vow'
x	's' in 'soon' (Note, **not** as an 'x')

13. Vietnamese Tones

As already mentioned and many of you will already know, Vietnamese is a tonal language, which means each word may be pronounced in different ways. In general, most people can understand what you are saying from the context, without using the tones – I myself was well understood living in Saigon without paying attention to most of the tones.

Although you can get by without using tones, if you are staying for any length of time, or if you would like to give the language a real go, it is worth spending a little time learning the tones. They are quite straight-forward and easy to use once you have learned them, because the tone of a word is indicated by a marking over or under each word.

I have attempted to describe the tones below, which is useful to read, but it will be even more useful to have a look and listen online – look up this video on Youtube demonstrating the tones, and there are many other videos too: http://www.youtube.com/watch?v=Rftv2o39Y3w).

No Tone (mid-level, flat) – No tone marker
This tone is easy – the syllable is said slightly higher than your most normal pitch (not low or high). The one thing to note, for completely correct pronunciation, is that the tone does not fall, which is the natural way to speak single words in English. Try it – say the word 'now' to yourself (or any word at all), and notice that your voice tone actually falls as you say the word. It is not a flat monotone – however, in Vietnamese, the correct pronunciation of syllables with no tone marker is really a flat monotone.

Mid-Level, Rising – Question mark (minus the dot) above the vowel
This is easy for English speakers – it is indicated in Vietnamese by a mini question mark above the vowel, and the pronunciation is just like the rising tone in English when we ask a question – think how you would pronounce "Me?" and this is the tone you are going for. A good example of this is the most famous Vietnamese dish, *phở*. The pronunciation of the word is [fuh?] including the question mark. This is tone is very easy to remember since the mini question mark above the syllable corresponds directly to our question tone too.

Mid-Level, Falling-then-Rising – Tilde (a.k.a. 'squiggly line') above the vowel
This tone is exactly what it says, falling, then rising, but when speaking, it can often sound like the 'Questioning tone' just mentioned but the syllable is extended. So for this one, we can take the simple question I mentioned above, "Me?" Now imagine that someone has just accused you of something and you really can't believe it. Try saying, "Me?" and drawing out the rising tone as you might in that context. Alternatively, just practice saying a syllable, "Me" is as good as any, at your normal pitch, and push your tone down and then up.

High-Rising – **A line above the vowel, which rises, from left to right (the acute accent in French)**
This is the same as the Mid-Level Rising tone, but that you pitch the word higher than your most normal pitch. So this is almost like a high-pitched questioning tone.

Low-Rising – A dot below the vowel
Just like with High-Rising, this is the same as the Mid-Level Rising tone, but obviously this one is pitched lower. It is effectively a low-pitched questioning tone.

Mid-Level, Falling – **A line above the vowel, which falls, from left to right. (the grave accent in French)**
Obviously, this is simply the opposite of the Mid-Level Rising Tone above. Here, you begin with your normal voice pitch and let it fall. This tone is how we speak single words in English. Remember above where I said to listen to yourself say a single word, e.g. "Now" – as you say an English word, your tone falls, and this is the tone required here. It is simply the same as when we say a single word in English.

Tips on Remembering the Tones

Contrary to Chinese and other languages, written Vietnamese assists even people who speak very little Vietnamese with being able to identify the tones because each tone has its own punctuation mark. You can always identify which tone a syllable uses by the marking above or below the syllable.

So, the way I remembered the tones, and found this very easy to do, was as follows (you may already find this straightforward, which it is, but this is simply to demystify the tones for anyone who may feel overwhelmed by all the markings):

- Aside from the 'No Tone' syllables, there are 5 tones.
- 4 out of 5 of the tones are effectively rising, so I found that easy to remember.
- There is only 1 Falling Tone.
- The 4 rising tones are indicated with markings that make good sense.
- The **Questioning** tone (Mid-Level Rising) is indicated by a **question mark**.
- The **High Rising** tone is indicated by a line which rises (from left to right) **above** the vowel.
- The **Low Rising** tone is indicated by a dot **below** the vowel.
- The **Falling-then-Rising** tone is indicated by the squiggly line (tilde) which itself **falls then rises**.
- The **Falling** tone is indicated by a line above the vowel which **falls** (from left to right).

As you can see, the tone markers have been chosen for a reason, and they indicate very simply for us which tone to use.

Also, if you are staying for any length of time and want to become proficient in the language, then it is not hard to arrange a language exchange with a student, where you teach them English and they teach you Vietnamese – practising with a native speaker will greatly improve your pronunciation and everyday vocabulary. Alternatively, there are tons of places you can sign up for Vietnamese classes, which is really the best way to learn the language if you want to become truly proficient. If you do a Google Search for Vietnamese language schools or Vietnamese language exchange in the city you will be in, you will be able to find something if you wish to.

14. A Summary of What You Will Need

In essence, this summary is simply reiterating the table of contents, but with slightly more detail. The intention is to highlight just how simple it is to build a working vocabulary in Vietnamese, which is sufficient to manage there for an extended period of time.

1. **Pronouns** – *I / we, 8 Pronouns,* + *các,* + *ấy,* + *của*
2. **Verbs** – *là, đi, muốn* etc + *không*
3. **Nouns & Adjectives** – a bare minimum needed to get by – you will naturally pick up more when you are there.
4. **Other Useful Phrases** – these will add deeper levels of meaning to your conversation.
5. **Question Words** – *gì, đâu, ai, tại sao, khi nào, như thế nào, bao nhiêu.*
6. **Basic Conversation Questions** – These will help you survive many conversations.
7. **Numbers & Counting** – including money, ordinal numbers and telling the time.
8. **Situational Vietnamese** – in a taxi, in a restaurant, in a coffee shop or bar, in a shop.
9. **Learning the tones** – the tones are actually not that difficult to learn and use, and will greatly enhance your Vietnamese.

15. Also Available

Please visit the Most Basic Languages website (mostbasiclanguages.com), where you will find the following (please note that if you are an early visitor, that I am right in the process of building this, and more is continually being added if you continue to check back):

Phone Applications:
- At least one FREE app for every language covered. More are being designed and produced to be free.
- Other inexpensive apps designed to bring the easily accessible language of these books (The Most Basic ____).
- Further apps designed to enhance your language learning experience, including exercise books / apps to complement these books, as well as more apps to improve your travel experience.

Travel Apps by Request:
We have been and are continuing to build apps as requested by you – anything you would love to see in an app related to languages, travel or living abroad, simply send an email to jim@mostbasiclanguages.com, and I will aim to have your app produced very quickly. It will then be made available cheaply for yourself and others to receive the benefits from.

*** This means that you can have any app you can think of to enhance your travel or language learning experience, within a couple of weeks of requesting it. ***

Other books:

- The Most Basic Chinese – All You Need to Know to Get By
The same structure and format as this book, but for Chinese. I lived in China for 2 years, and this basically contains all of the language I needed to live there.

- The Most Vital Chinese & The Most Vital Vietnamese
These two short e-booklets, outline days, dates and the vocabulary needed for staying in a hotel in China and Vietnam, and which I try to make **free** to download on Amazon on the 1st and 15th of each month.

More to come:

- More "**The Most Basic ____**" language books and apps to come. I am currently working with people on a number of other languages to expand the series, as well as converting the series into Android and IOS Applications which will also include the ability to listen to the pronunciation of a native speaker. Please keep an eye out for these in the near future if you are interested.

16. Final Note

One of the great things about visiting Vietnam is that people come away with such varied opinions and experiences – some feel they cannot handle the 'hassle' they receive at the hands of some of the people who make their living from tourists, others come across many wonderful, friendly and generous locals, some stick only to the main tourist drags, some try to get off the beaten track (which can seem difficult there).

For me, I have seen both sides, but I have personally found that, apart from the various people who make their living from tourists, the Vietnamese people can be among the friendliest, warmest and most charming of anywhere I have been. It is a real shame that the vast majority of visitors only really experience those tourist touts and come away with a negative impression of the people – the Vietnamese themselves are attempting to deal with this issue and feel much shame in their reputation being tarnished by a very visible minority.

If you can, I would highly recommend getting off the main tourist trail, and you will have the chance to meet some really great people. So my advice is to make this small effort to learn a little of the language, and you will greatly enhance the enjoyment of your time in Vietnam!

Have a great trip!

All rights reserved © James McGlasson, 2012

Printed in Poland
by Amazon Fulfillment
Poland Sp. z o.o., Wrocław